duck

chicken

horse

stable

sheep

Count the farmyard animals and objects and find them in the picture. Trace over the numbers, then colour in the farmyard.

Name the colours, trace over the words
and colour in the farmyard.

yellow

green

black

purple

pink

red

Can you find the opposites in the farmyard? Trace over the words and find them in the picture. Then colour in the farmyard.

high	low
big	small
tall	short
heavy	light
in	out
wet	dry
awake	asleep
black	white

This is what the farmyard looks like throughout the year.
How many seasons are there? Can you name them?

spring

winter

Trace over the words, and then colour in the farmyard.

summer

autumn

Here are some opposite words to trace over.
Colour in the pictures and see how they are opposite.

big
small

tall
short

fast
slow

high
low

stop
go